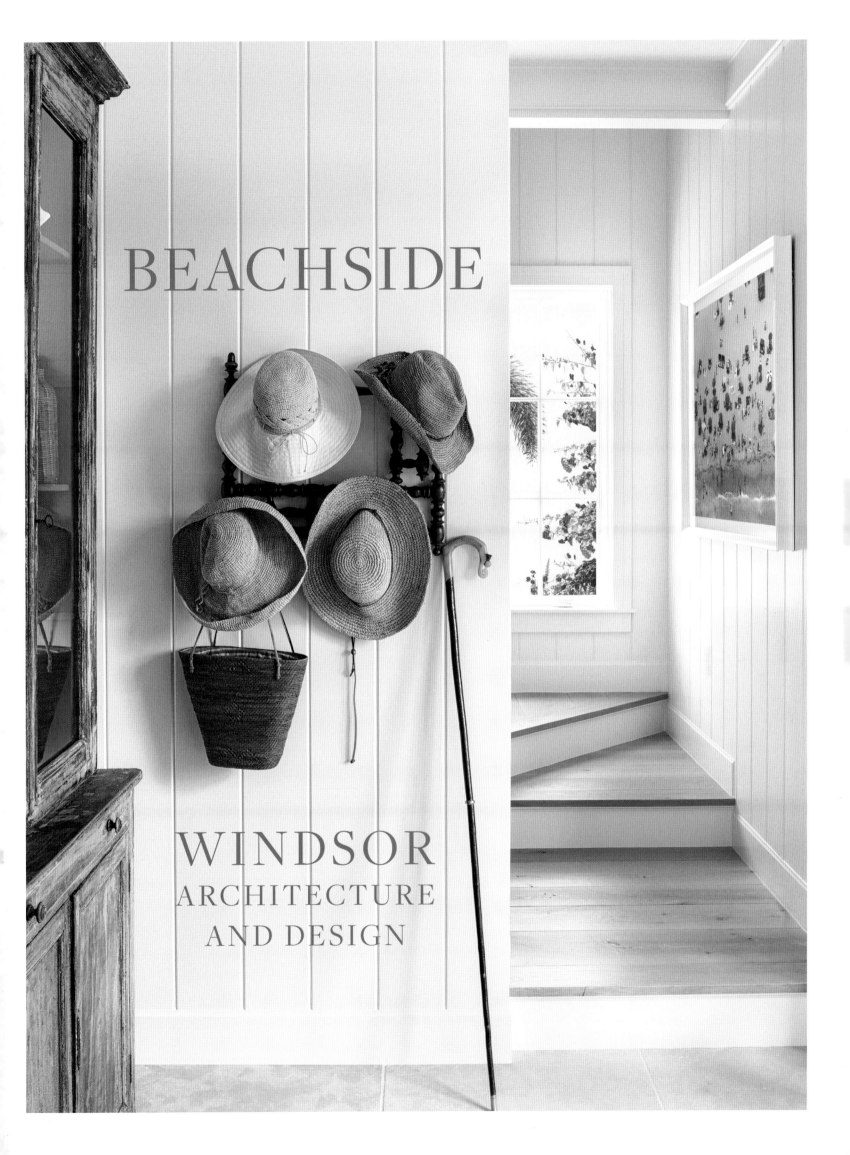

BEACHSIDE

WINDSOR
ARCHITECTURE
AND DESIGN

BEACHSIDE

WINDSOR
ARCHITECTURE
AND DESIGN

HADLEY KELLER

INTRODUCTION BY
JAMES REGINATO

PHOTOGRAPHY BY
JESSICA KLEWICKI GLYNN

VENDOME

NEW YORK • LONDON

Contents

Introduction
JAMES REGINATO

I t all began more than thirty years ago, when W. Galen and Hilary M. Weston searched for respite from another frigid Toronto winter for themselves and their children. "We're snowbirds, so we decided to come to Florida and find along this wonderful, big coastline a place where we could put our feet down," Mrs. Weston said recently, recounting the genesis of Windsor, the extraordinary residential sporting community that the couple founded in 1989.

Notwithstanding Mrs. Weston's modest tone, she and her husband thought big—on a scale consistent with all their endeavors. Before his death in 2021, Galen owned or controled hundreds of companies through George Weston Limited, the Toronto-based conglomerate founded by his grandfather in 1882. He was also Chairman Emeritus of Selfridges Group, which includes Selfridges & Co in the U.K. and Holt Renfrew in Canada.

Hilary, born in Ireland, is one of Canada's most influential women, recognized for her philanthropic work, business acumen, and public service. From 1997 to 2002, she served as Lieutenant Governor of Ontario, the British Crown's constitutional representative in the province. (We should properly address her, therefore, as the Hon. Hilary M. Weston.)

The place the Westons found to put their feet down turned out to be 472 idyllic acres on a lush barrier island between the Indian River and the Atlantic Ocean, in Vero Beach (ninety minutes north of Palm Beach), where subtropical and tropical climates mingle.

"It was still citrus groves and bungalows, dirt roads and wooden walkways, totally unspoiled. We thought, we could make it into something very special," Mrs. Weston recalls.

The Westons envisioned instead a village-like community that would be developed along the lines of the New Urbanism, then a nascent urban planning movement advocating for walkable, compact cities with a consistent architectural style. Despite the "New" in its name, the ideology is rooted in classicism and traditional architecture along a European model.

Mr. and Mrs. Weston had first learned about this movement when the Prince of Wales introduced them to Léon Krier, the Luxembourg-born urban planner and

architect who has been recognized as the founding father of New Urbanism; Krier conceived the plan for Poundbury, the new town in Dorset, England, initiated by Prince Charles.

After discussions with Krier, the Westons went to see New Urbanism's leading American proponents, the husband-and-wife duo of Andrés Duany and Elizabeth Plater-Zyberk, who had just launched their firm, Duany Plater-Zyberk & Company (now DPZ CoDesign), in Miami. On the drawing boards were plans for Seaside, the first pedestrian-focused community in Florida.

"They were young and great fun; in them we found kindred spirits," Hilary recalls of her first meeting with the couple, whom the Westons promptly hired to draw up the master plan for Windsor and create what would become known as the Windsor Code, a handbook that delineates the permitted architectural elements. Drawing on the traditional styles found in such locales as Charleston, South Carolina, and the British West Indies—where houses feature large porches and courtyards—an Anglo-Caribbean style was chosen for Windsor.

"The Westons actually took a tremendous risk," Duany recently recalled. "There are many of these communities now, but at the time it was pioneering."

Initially, sport provided an organizing and animating principal for Windsor (which drew its name from the royal town in England, where Mrs. Weston also maintains a family home). A world-class polo field was laid out, where players at the spirited matches included Mr. Weston and his son, Galen Jr., as well as visitors such as Prince Charles. Then came the eighteen-hole links-style championship golf course designed by Robert Trent Jones Jr. This sporting paradise grew to accommodate all manner of equestrian and aquatic pursuits, as well as nearly anything involving a racket or a mallet.

At the heart of it is the Village Centre, which features an old-fashioned village green, a general store, a post office, the Windsor Suites (a collection of seven guest accommodations), the Concierge, and an amphitheater designed for concerts and special events. Everything at Windsor radiates from this center. Some 350 homesites are laid out along a series of pleasant, tree-lined streets, as well as along the ocean.

Though there are a variety of building types—village houses, cottages, county estates—their sizes, heights, and styles are strictly regulated by the Windsor Code. Distinctive features include steeply pitched metal or wood roofs, open eaves with exposed rafter tails, vertically proportioned windows and doors, cantilevered balconies, small windowpanes, and exterior walls in neutral colors.

Because Windsor's ways were novel at first, the Westons constructed several showhouses; Hilary served as master contractor and design director. "Some people came and didn't know what we were doing. Others got it right away," she recalls of the community's early days. "We put in the infrastructure and then there was no stopping us. We had great fun, but we were pretty serious in the sense that we never changed our direction. Our idea was to make something that was appropriate here, on the best coastline in Southern Florida."

The Windsor "look" also gained momentum through the dreamy Beach Club, which was designed by architect Jaquelin Robertson, a Virginia-born patrician, with original décor by Naomi Leff, whose interiors for Ralph Lauren's flagship store on Madison Avenue in Manhattan were so influential.

The elegant yet casual style Robertson and Neff created (later freshened by South Florida designer Rod Mickley), set a tone for Windsor. "People took their lead from what they saw there. It provided inspiration for people as they designed their own homes," says Mrs. Weston. The same could be said of Windsor's other public buildings—including the Clubhouse, designed by architect Clemens Bruns Schaub, with original interiors by Yabu Pushelberg—as well as the oceanfront house that the Westons built for themselves, in collaboration with Clemens Bruns Schaub and interior designer John Stefanidis. A study in elegant simplicity, it features a vast second-story great room with a high, white-painted king-post ceiling, French doors adorned with blue-and-white tulle curtains, and stone floors.

The 1990s, when Windsor was getting off the ground, was a time of great adventure, Mrs. Weston recalls. "Every day about four in the afternoon we'd take a walk and could peek into what everyone was building. People followed the code and embraced it, but each house was unique. Nothing is a copy of anything else."

ABOVE
Windsor's oceanfront homes are nestled among sand dunes and sea grass.

Unlike many other Floridian gated communities, which are inhabited predominantly by retirees, Windsor has always been multi-generational. Consequently, its population has grown quite organically. A number of young adults who grew up here have married each other—including Galen Jr., who was wed in 2005 to Alexandra Schmidt, daughter of another Toronto family who winters in Windsor. Over the years, the community's Town Hall, a masterpiece designed by Léon Krier in 1999, has been the site of numerous weddings between Windsor families. "That's something we hoped for," says Mrs. Weston, with a twinkle in her eye.

Even better, many of these happy young couples have built their own homes in the community, bringing to Windsor a new generation of smart designers with fresh ideas.

Altogether, over three decades, the community has been built by a dream team of architects and designers. "Windsor looks like an authentic town because it is designed by many hands," says Duany.

Though Windsor's public buildings have been featured in many publications, the private side has not been widely seen—until now. *Beachside* pulls back the curtain, as it were, to highlight for the first time the domestic world of Windsor: the houses. Thanks to the perceptive lens of photographer Jessica Klewicki Glynn and the keen reportage of author Hadley Keller, these pages reveal the stylistic gamut that runs through the enclave.

The range of styles might surprise some readers—particularly those who assumed that Windsor's strict code would carry over to what lies behind the walls. In fact, the architectural guidelines have challenged designers to find ways to break the mold inside. New York–based interior designer Steven Gambrel, for example, looked to Morocco when he designed a house for a young couple who told him they wanted something with a very exotic flair. "They were looking to go far, far away," he recounts. "I didn't feel at all restricted by the Windsor Code. Nor did my clients. On the contrary, the big, deep porches and courtyards gave me opportunities to create outdoor rooms; and although the architecture is reminiscent of period houses, the interiors are large, open spaces, so you don't feel restricted in terms of scale or volume. Because the spaces are so big and generous, they are easy to decorate."

Three decades on, Windsor's final phase is underway. Construction has begun in the new North Village neighborhood, with its thirty-six homesites set on forty-seven acres, all being master-planned once again by DPZ.

"Here we are, thirty years later," says Mrs. Weston, with a mixture of pride and slight surprise. "We never lost sight of our vision. It has developed absolutely the way we wanted, because we didn't compromise, we took our time—and we had terrific architects and designers."

Entrances and Stair Halls

To enter any home at Windsor is to step into something of a secret garden.

"Privacy," the project's planner Andrés Duany once said, "is the greatest luxury." In a community that fiercely values this luxury, gates and hedges serve not only as the protective casings of personal lives but also as the elegant exoskeletons that beget a perpetual sense of arrival. "It's this sort of Alice in Wonderland effect," says architect Clemens Bruns Schaub—who designed the first cluster of homes in the community and has gone on to build dozens more—of the experience of strolling through Windsor's streets and buildings.

Thanks to the careful planning inherent in Duany and Elizabeth Plater-Zyberk's (DPZ CoDesign) New Urbanism philosophy, each square foot of land at Windsor is painstakingly arranged in a way that gently guides the eye and creates a natural, beckoning flow—but always, too, a delightful dose of the unexpected.

"Everything is meant to please the guest, to make it comfortable but also surprising," says the Rome-born, Chicago-based interior designer Alessandra Branca, who renovated Windsor's guest suites in 2018, extending DPZ's philosophy to even the most short-term visitors. "It's very similar to the kind of urban living in a city like Rome—you have intimate public streets and then courtyards where people have their private lives."

New Urbanism is, after all, rooted in classicism, a connecting thread that ensures continuity as well as human-centric design. "The proportions are so elegant and timeless because they're based on classical principles," says Chris Baker of Moor, Baker & Associates, another architectural firm that has designed many Windsor homes. "And I think the human spirit really responds to those proportions."

Indeed, the community's strict architectural guidelines, albeit sometimes a creative hurdle to architects ("The model is not for the faint of heart," quips Simon Jacobsen, partner at Jacobsen Architecture, the firm founded by his father, Hugh Newell Jacobsen, which has created several homes there), challenge the most enterprising architects to find pleasing ways to break the mold.

OPPOSITE

With its turned-concrete columns and central fountain, Scott Merrill compares this courtyard to one at a Pompeian house. Landscape designer Dan Ford selected the lush plantings, which lend a layered texture to the atrium.

"Go anyplace that is really beautiful—say Nantucket or Florence—and I think you'll find that the buildings share a commonality," says Moor, Baker's Peter Moor. "But the cool parts of all those places are the little things that deviate from that commonality." Take a spin through Windsor and you'll be well aware that you're in a planned community, of course, but you'll also find your eye drawn to the charismatic variance in the ostensibly repeating façades.

DPZ's overarching concept extends from the public spaces to the private—pathways and open areas and boundaries are reprised on a smaller scale in a sort of matryoshka doll effect. Bougainvillea-covered pergolas make way to brick-paved exterior enfilades, sleepy slatted shutters open to reveal sun-drenched courtyards. Each window, archway, or open door offers a peek at the private lives within.

"I used to love going out on my bicycle or for a walk at nine o'clock in the evening, when everyone was back home from dinner, so I could see into everyone's homes all lit up," recalls the Sydney-based American designer Thomas Hamel, who has been working on a home for clients at Windsor for the past decade. "I love taking in every window and gate—you can really be such a voyeur."

Once inside, of course, architects and designers have freer rein and, thanks to the famously aesthetically minded residents of Windsor, are happily afforded the canvas to express it. "The people there really love architecture, really love the process," says Ashley Olivia Waddell, who, with her sister, Courtney O'Bryan Harris, runs Olivia O'Bryan, a Vero Beach–based interior design firm that has decorated numerous Windsor homes.

A prime example? For one family's fourth house in the community, where years of practiced design patronage led to a heightened sense of adventure, Waddell and Harris, in partnership with Moor, Baker, designed a modern serpentine stair that appears almost as a plaster sculpture emerging from the wall behind it.

The formal entrance hall of a home decorated by Nassau-based interior designer Amanda Lindroth, meanwhile, is swathed in mint-green lattice, an apt introduction to the playful—yet formal—space within. In the vestibule of a home designed by Steven Gambrel, an orange-and-magenta artwork beckons, an energizing departure from the muted Windsor exteriors.

In the glass-walled entry at the home of some of Hugh Newell Jacobsen's best clients, a transparent spiral staircase appears suspended over a cerulean orb by Anish Kapoor, affording the owners—and lucky houseguests—a view many museumgoers would only dream of.

These are, after all, dream houses—often for both client and designer. Largely unencumbered by much of the more banal functionality of a primary residence, homes at Windsor are, instead, artful expressions of their residents and designers set within the thoughtful framework of the New Urbanist ideal.

The entrances are just the very beginning—welcome in.

OPPOSITE
Even homes without oceanfront placement often sit waterside, thanks to strategically placed pools and ponds.

OVERLEAF
Houses at Windsor are typically built around courtyards, a layout that affords a unique privacy and often, as exemplified by this Clemens Bruns Schaub home, a dramatic sense of arrival.

OPPOSITE

Beguiling exterior pathways like this one, lined with verdant hedges and tropical plantings, connect outdoor spaces.

ABOVE

Twin staircases provide easy access to the courtyard even from the second floor; well-positioned foliage adds dimension to the façade.

ABOVE

Pergolas, a frequent sight at Windsor, provide support for climbing flora and create elegant approaches to front doors.

OPPOSITE

Interior designer Alessandra Branca lined the pathway to the Windsor guest suites with a canopy of trees so that "you walk through a garden to get to your suite."

OVERLEAF

Hugh Newell Jacobsen's trademark square windowpanes are here balanced with slatted Bermuda shutters, a nod to the community's Anglo-Caribbean influence.

OPPOSITE

George Pastor outfitted a home adjacent to Windsor's Equestrian Centre with gracefully arched, mahogany Dutch doors, easy to open for a light breeze—or an equine visitor.

ABOVE

Tall palm trees anchor the corners of the courtyard at the same Pastor house—and guide the eye to the Equestrian Centre, visible through the far doors.

ABOVE

Architects Moor, Baker emphasize the indoor-outdoor ethos of the community with an enfilade of arched openings connecting courtyard to interior to exterior.

OPPOSITE

A large part of the allure of the courtyard style is the enticing glimpses of the houses' inner sanctums from the outside.

ENTRANCES AND STAIR HALLS

LEFT

Set at the water's edge, a home by Clemens Bruns Schaub appears to float above the waterfall beside it.

OVERLEAF

The architecture and landscape design of Windsor's best homes, like this one by Clemens Bruns Schaub, share equal billing.

PAGES 42–43

At the same Schaub house, tropical flora grace the entry, amplifying the sense of arrival.

ABOVE
Windsor's earliest houses, like this one by Gibson & Associates, are clearly Anglo-Caribbean in style, with stucco walls and slatted shutters in pastel hues.

OPPOSITE
The community's building code stipulates open eaves, vertically proportioned windows, and cantilevered balconies, as seen here.

OVERLEAF
As the community has grown, architects have pushed the boundaries of the code, as illustrated by this Moor, Baker–designed residence, where Windsor's standard layout meets Moorish influence.

ENTRANCES AND STAIR HALLS

3130

OPPOSITE

In the entrance hall of this Moor, Baker and Olivia O'Bryan house, a sculptural spiral staircase deviates from the Windsor architectural "norm."

ABOVE

Window frames and muntins in black wrought iron are a modern, industrial departure from the Anglo-Caribbean style.

OVERLEAF

Sunlight pours into a neutral-toned entryway by Vero Beach design firm Olivia O'Bryan, where quiet calm is the order of the day.

ABOVE
In this entry, a subtle, studded detail on the walls reflects the nailhead trim on the settee.

OPPOSITE
At a home by Merrill, Pastor & Colgan, sunlight pours into a double-height entry, making an elegant first impression.

OVERLEAF LEFT
In a house designed by Hugh Newell Jacobsen, an unassuming hallway becomes a de facto gallery when lined with the resident's art collection.

OVERLEAF RIGHT
Jacobsen designed a cantilevered spiral stair that swirls above a cerulean sculpture by Anish Kapoor in the house's entryway.

ABOVE
Despite its seaside locale, Windsor's interiors aren't always beachy, as illustrated by this stair hall with its hardwood floor, campaign desk, and Regency-style mirror.

OPPOSITE
Art is a staple in nearly all Windsor homes. This red canvas is by Sir Christopher Le Brun, a British painter who exhibited at the Windsor gallery in 2017.

ABOVE

In a home inspired by Morocco, interior designer Steven Gambrel set the colorful tone for the interiors in the entry, where a bright, boldly patterned textile hangs on a plaster wall.

OPPOSITE

Textures collide in the hallway of a Payette & Payette house decorated by Rod Mickley, featuring terra-cotta floors, plaster demilune tables, a graphically patterned runner, and mirrors framed in undulating rattan.

OPPOSITE

In the entry of an otherwise colorful home, interior designer Lindsey Coral Harper eases into bright hues with touches of pink on a lantern and side table.

ABOVE

Across from the peacock chair (opposite), a Hunt Slonem bird painting greets visitors to the Coral Harper–designed home; practical stools for shoe removal are tucked under the entry table.

OVERLEAF LEFT

A lattice wall facing the courtyard of an Olivia O'Bryan house has the feel of a beach cabana.

OVERLEAF RIGHT

Interior designer Amanda Lindroth offers up a joyful take on trellising in a fresh mint green for homeowners who wanted a home that felt fun— but still formal.

OPPOSITE

In the Westons' home, John Stefanidis gave a staircase an artful touch with floral cutouts, which cast beguiling shadows on the floor below.

ABOVE

Stefanidis's sherbet palette keeps the interiors of the Westons' house from feeling too serious—despite a proliferation of art and collectible furniture.

Living Rooms

To invoke the term *happy place* in reference to a vacation home is, admittedly, to scrape the bottom of a writer's cliché barrel, but that term is, quite simply, the most common descriptor among designers and inhabitants of houses at Windsor.

"People always come into my home and say, 'This is such a happy house," says the designer Britt Taner, who has created two homes at Windsor for her young family, both quite minimal architecturally, but shot through with pattern and color—like a living room anchored by a sofa upholstered in Josef Frank's jovial Citrus Garden fabric and a tomato-red lacquer sideboard, or a family room with furniture and walls swathed in Colefax and Fowler's iconic Bowood chintz.

"The colors I use here are happy colors, and the house is very happy, very uplifting, and, most of all, really comfortable," echoes designer Susan Zises Green, who outfitted her own homes at Windsor with a collection of furniture pulled from prior residences, resulting in a sort of greatest hits of the designer's own interior style.

"Second homes are my favorite jobs, because I think the clients are always a little bit more free," says Lindsey Coral Harper, who has designed two Windsor homes. After all, she adds, "This is their escape—they want it to be a fun place, a place where they can enjoy every minute."

About the home she designed for a couple from Montreal, Amanda Lindroth says, "We wanted the house to have a particular sense of whimsy, a crazy light-hearted, timeless resort feeling," a balance achieved through a meeting of exuberant color with serious antiques. Lindroth's clients intended to use it as a temporary dwelling while constructing their dream home—but wound up so enchanted with it that those plans are on indefinite hold.

It bears emphasizing that the best Windsor homes—like the best homes anywhere—are the most personal, reflecting not only the residents' tastes but their unique personalities, lives, and sensibilities. That may be the reason they run such a stylistic gamut, despite the strict architectural parameters.

For some residents, finding that personal connection might mean evoking a favorite far-flung destination, as New York-based designer Steven Gambrel did for a family that had been inspired by frequent travel to Morocco. To evoke the feel of Marrakech and Tangier, Gambrel infused the space with rich hues and imported mirrors and light fixtures from the Middle East—a striking departure from the neutral façades outside. "We love the style at Windsor, but we wanted to create a home that allowed you to feel as though you had stepped into an unexpected land," explains the designer of the riad-inspired abode.

For others, this might simply mean filling homes with the most personal of effects, reimagining family heirlooms or favorite furnishings from previous homes within a new context. "Most of the community's members move there for the winter, or longer," observes Alessandra Branca. "So it's not just a two-week vacation in the Caribbean" but a home in which you want to be surrounded by your own things. "You want to mix them in."

Central to that mix for many is art. The Westons themselves set the tone; works from their own collection are spread throughout their home, as well as Windsor's clubhouse and gallery. Members follow suit: Visitors to the home of one of Harper's clients are met with a massive Hunt Slonem canvas in the entry, followed by an exuberantly colored Mel Bochner work in the dining room. In one cozy home, nearly every square inch of wall space is covered with an eclectic mix of paintings (the works are even hung across the living room bookshelves). In a Schaub-designed living room, a full-wall multicolor canvas is a richer alternative to a wallpaper.

Of course, any designer with a healthy sense of place is quick to note that, even as backdrop to the most blue-chip collections, it is often the natural surroundings that take center stage here. "Every view out of a window is very, very important," says Simon Jacobsen, whose firm's multiple Windsor projects house works by the likes of Ellsworth Kelly, Maya Lin, and Deborah Butterfield (plus the aforementioned Anish Kapoor).

Maximizing those views is a core tenet of the Jacobsens' work at Windsor. "You'll see, say, that a pavilion will suddenly change direction, sort of seemingly without reason," says the architect. "The reason is that if we didn't do it, we'd be looking at the parking space, and rotating 45 degrees allows us to look out over water."

At the home he designed for a modernism-loving, design-savvy client, Brad Lynch took that concept to its aesthetic extreme with an open-plan living space separated from its courtyard by just a sheet of floor-to-ceiling glass. "It's always about the relationship to the site and the natural landscape," says the principal of Chicago-based Brininstool & Lynch of the home, which pushes Windsor's design code toward modernism more than perhaps any other building there. "The area that we had to work with wasn't huge, but it offered an opportunity to create this balance between indoor and outdoor space. The idea was, whenever you're inside you have a constant emphasis on the outdoors."

OPPOSITE
The courtyard view and plentiful sunlight in this study make it the perfect spot for painting, a passion the owner shares with her daughter.

OVERLEAF
A large-scale Alex Katz portrait overlooks the living room in a house decorated by Rod Mickley. The room also features several works by Christo and Jeanne-Claude.

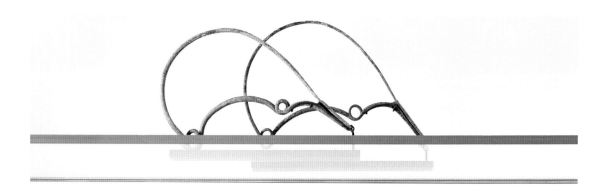

ABOVE

In an art-filled home by Hugh Newell Jacobsen, every last small-scale sculpture has its place on the living room's shelves. "Hugh thinks of everything," says the homeowner.

OPPOSITE

Thanks to floor-to-ceiling glass panels, the courtyard of this Jacobsen-designed home appears almost as an extension of the living room.

OVERLEAF

The living room is outfitted with iconic mid-century furniture as well as tables of Jacobsen's own design, all against the backdrop of his trademark square-paned windows.

PRECEDING PAGES

A sculptural plaster chimney breast makes an elegant centerpiece in the living room of an airy home by Moor, Baker & Associates and Olivia O'Bryan.

RIGHT

For a Morocco-loving family, Steven Gambrel channeled the spirit of Tangier with textiles and plaster walls in saturated colors, as well as a Moroccan chandelier.

OPPOSITE AND ABOVE

Josef Frank's exuberant Citrus Garden fabric was the jumping-off point for the living room in designer Britt Taner's family home. Lacquered lampshades and a sideboard in tomato red give a jolt to the room, whose barn-style architecture is fairly bare-boned.

OVERLEAF

A wall of African acacia conceals storage and provides an organic backdrop for modern furniture in a living room by architect Brad Lynch for a design-savvy family.

ABOVE
Landon Mackenzie's Point of Entry (Ice Track)*—inspired by an Arctic ice floe—makes a bold statement in a living room outfitted with modern furniture.*

OPPOSITE
The convex mirror above the fireplace was purchased from the Florentine studio Flare and had to be shipped to Windsor in a custom crate (it measures 58 inches in diameter).

OVERLEAF
A pair of vintage Arne Jacobsen Swan chairs (1958) face the Landon Mackenzie work in the white-walled living room.

ABOVE

A colorful lamp sits on a table in the living room of interior designer Susan Zises Green's own Windsor home, which is full of furniture she's collected over the years.

OPPOSITE

"I used colors I don't usually use for myself," says Zises Green of the proliferation of pinks and yellows, which, she says, "are happy colors."

OVERLEAF

The centerpiece of Zises Green's living room is a large world map that she recovered from the old offices of 20th Century Fox in New York (her father owned the building).

Dining Rooms and Kitchens

Anyone who says the open-plan concept has killed the formal dining room need only pay a visit to Windsor to observe that the tradition of real, sit-down dining is alive and well. Even in homes with the eat-in islands ubiquitous in today's kitchens, just round a corner and you'll almost always find a traditional dining table too. Usually, these eating areas are situated so as to offer up the very best of the house's views—call it Windsor's take on dinner and a show—and often even extend to the outdoors, blurring the lines between inside and out in true Windsor fashion.

In the Westons' John Stefanidis–designed home, vaulted white ceilings frame the ocean vista beyond, while a massive square dining table of carved stone accommodates many dinner guests, not to mention exuberant centerpieces. At a Clemens Bruns Schaub and Thomas Hamel–designed abode influenced by Southeast Asia, living room doors open out to a poolside dining table set beneath a minimal pergola. Even in an Olivia O'Bryan–designed home with a spacious, eat-in kitchen, a long dining table gets pride of place in the open great room beneath a glittering chandelier, its shape guiding the eye to the pool beyond.

That's not to say these spaces take themselves too seriously, though—this is vacation living, after all. That oversized table in the Westons' home gets a dash of playfulness by way of sculptural chairs in a variety of bright hues (which fold up for easy rearranging), while floor-to-ceiling banana-leaf wallpaper in the dining room of an architecturally minimal Jacobsen home gives the space a tropical garden party vibe. A multicolor bubble chandelier and bold abstract art above an otherwise all-white dining area evoke a retro feel.

In one unconventional approach to the formal dining room, the homeowner filled the shelves that line the walls—which had been populated by the previous owners with entertaining-adjacent decorative objects—with books, turning the room into a combination library and eating area.

Stylistically disparate though they may be, each of these interpretations reinforces the core principles of the traditional dining room: meals as a time to gather and as an occasion in and of themselves. "They entertain in an old-fashioned way," says Amanda Lindroth of clients for whom she relocated the dining room into the more spacious former living room to offer up greater seating capacity for dinner parties. She then took it one step further, transforming what was billed as a downstairs bedroom into the ultimate host's amenity: "They were using it as a storage area, so we turned it into a party cupboard," she says.

Such an approach toward stowing entertaining accoutrements is apt at Windsor, where homes are tasked with metaphorically shrinking and expanding, depending on the occasion. While at Christmas a home might be abuzz with dozens of nieces and nephews, children, and other assorted relatives and friends, it must not feel cavernous and echoing once these guests depart.

"When I first visited, I thought it was such a big house," confesses Susan Zises Green of her current Windsor home, an upsize from her first in the community. "But then it just got smaller and smaller in my mind. And now, even when I'm in it alone, I find it cozy."

That may be why even the homes with the grandest formal dining rooms often also boast spacious kitchen islands, intimate breakfast nooks, or tables drawn up to comfy banquettes, where dining can feel just as fabulous for a smaller group. In a kitchen by interior designer Leah Muller, a graphic wallpaper and woven stools keep stainless appliances and crisp, white cabinetry from feeling cold. In a Schaub-designed one, meanwhile, a bold blue artwork overlooking graphic counter stools in a similar hue is sure to elevate even the most lowbrow takeout cartons.

For residents who love to cook, kitchens, like the rest of the house, are conceived with the perfect balance between functional ease and stylistic expression. If you're going to be washing dishes, the task is ever so much more pleasant if the sink overlooks a courtyard pool. If you're in need of somewhere to corral your collection of pots and pans, make it a sculptural overhead pot rack topped with potted plants. Or, take the expression of form and function to the extreme, as in the case of one Thomas Hamel–designed kitchen—or, rather, two Thomas Hamel–designed kitchens: a display one with handsome stools and chic pendants and a prep one, tucked away behind a far wall.

OPPOSITE
Lindsey Coral Harper pulled the green hue of the dining chairs' upholstery from the Mel Bochner painting behind them; the palm frond pendant is a festive topper.

OVERLEAF LEFT
Many Windsor homes have French doors that can be thrown open to extend dining spaces to the outdoors.

OVERLEAF RIGHT
An assortment of small-scale drawings makes an impactful statement when grouped on the wall of this traditional dining area.

OPPOSITE

A massive, cut-stone table is the centerpiece of the Westons' John Stefanidis–designed dining area; colorful folding dining chairs are easily portable to accommodate more or fewer guests.

ABOVE

On the Westons' tabletop, Raynaud's coral-patterned Cristobal porcelain by Alberto Pinto brings a touch of tropical whimsy alongside formal silver and glassware.

ABOVE
The owner of this house, an avid collector of tabletop décor, mixes contemporary pieces with antique silver and linens for elegant settings that aren't fussy.

OPPOSITE
She filled the built-in shelves lining her dining room with colorful books, giving it the feel of an eat-in library.

DINING ROOMS AND KITCHENS

OPPOSITE AND ABOVE

A native Midwesterner, designer Britt Taner wanted her Windsor home to feel like a modern spin on a barn, a look she achieved with Wheeler Kearns Architects. A rustic wood tabletop reinforces the barn sensibility, while a colorful sideboard and abstract art give the room a modern pop.

OPPOSITE

A glittering chandelier hangs from the double-height ceiling above a long dining table in a Moor, Baker & Associates and Olivia O'Bryan–designed home. Upholstery in varying shades breaks up the uniformity of the ten dining chairs.

ABOVE

In the monochromatic kitchen of the same house, texture is the focus; glass tile, white marble, and a plaster hood keep the space light.

OVERLEAF

Olivia O'Bryan's Ashley Olivia Waddell and Courtney O'Bryan Harris strung a sculptural counterbalance pendant by Florian Schulz over the island to add dimension and dynamism to the all-white kitchen.

OPPOSITE

A large-scale painting by Gert & Uwe Tobias hangs over the kitchen table in this Clemens Bruns Schaub–designed home. A wood-grain ceiling adds warmth.

ABOVE

A trio of pendants by Roost swirl above counter stools that pick up the colors in the Tobias work across the room.

OPPOSITE

Comprised of thirty-seven hand-blown orbs, a multicolor chandelier by Omer Arbel (which requires its own ceiling support) reflects the tones in paintings by Michael Adamson.

ABOVE

Each of the Windsor guest suites—designed by Alessandra Branca—has a dedicated color scheme. The pink suite features abstract artwork by Catherine Booker Jones.

ABOVE
CW Stockwell's lush Martinique wallpaper is a delightful foil to the clean lines of a Hugh Newell Jacobsen–designed house.

OPPOSITE
Light filtering through a series of French doors casts a warm glow along an interior enfilade.

ABOVE

In lieu of a single large fixture, interior designer Thomas Hamel opted for a quintet of Tom Dixon pendants over the table in this "show" kitchen. A second, prep, kitchen is tucked behind the back wall.

OPPOSITE

A table set poolside under a pergola just off the kitchen extends the dining (and entertaining) area of this Thomas Hamel home from indoors to out.

OVERLEAF

Architect Brad Lynch carefully calibrated the placement of interior walls and furniture to align with the double reflecting pools in the courtyard of this modern house.

ABOVE
Sight lines inside the house are just as important to Lynch; here, a sculptural table is visible across the ground floor.

OPPOSITE
The long, linear island in the kitchen echoes the shape of the painting, which the residents commissioned from Buenos Aires–based artist Fernando O'Connor.

OVERLEAF
In an Olivia O'Bryan–decorated house designed with Merrill, Pastor & Colgan, the living, kitchen, and dining areas converge under a vaulted ceiling.

VANITY FAIR PORTRAITS

POOLSIDE WITH SLIM AARONS

ABOVE

In the breakfast nook at the far end of the room on the preceding pages, windows open up to lush tropical greenery.

OPPOSITE

Another Olivia O'Bryan–designed kitchen features a ceiling in pale blue, the shade common on porch ceilings in the American South, rooted in the Creole tradition of warding off evil spirits.

OVERLEAF

The patterned tile on the walls of a Leah Muller–designed kitchen lends a textural effect in keeping with the woven-rattan counter stools.

PRECEDING PAGES
In a kitchen designed by Tom Scheerer, a cheerful yellow tile backsplash from Cuban Tropical Tile pairs well with open cabinets backed in Benjamin Moore's Bird's Egg blue, a striking backdrop for assorted white serving dishes.

OPPOSITE
In this kitchen, a dramatic stainless-steel pot rack is topped with an array of houseplants to add texture.

ABOVE
Ever party-ready, the same kitchen houses a collection of silver, both collected and inherited from family.

OVERLEAF
Low-slung sofas lend a relaxed vibe to the seating area off of the kitchen in this Steven Gambrel–designed home, the décor of which was inspired by Morocco.

Family Rooms and Studies

If the living and dining rooms at Windsor are the open, exuberant gathering spaces of the houses, they are balanced by the rarer cozy study or family room, which, depending on the occasion, might act as an extension of a hosting space—or a blessed escape from it.

Windsor's courtyard style means that these spaces are often cleverly tucked into corners, making use of the few walls that don't open up to a yard or through to an exterior vista.

"The code sort of leads architects toward houses that are one room deep," says Clemens Bruns Schaub. "Tropical houses by their very nature are about that cross ventilation, that light, that proximity to outdoors."

In an inverse of most houses, then, the spaces *without* striking views and easy outdoor access have a certain kind of special allure. As a result, designers and residents often take the opportunity to treat the decoration of these rooms differently, turning them into hidden jewel boxes.

In one den, the walls, doors, and ceiling are lacquered in a delicious salmon hue, casting a warm glow that would hardly be possible with windows larger than the narrow band of them in this room. Or, consider a study by interior designer Liz Eubank, who covered built-in shelves with a midnight-blue lacquer, creating a dramatic backdrop for the collected objects displayed on them. Britt Taner took a different approach in her family room, swathing walls and sectional sofa alike in Colefax and Fowler's iconic Bowood chintz for a cocooning effect.

It's easy to imagine sneaking away to one of these spaces for a quiet moment, whether to work, converse, or enjoy a book—or a nightcap. That allure, of course, is all, quite literally, part of the plan. "What the Windsor plan does really well is take relatively small lots but make them really generous with space," says Scott Merrill, who helped to develop the Windsor design code after working with DPZ on Seaside, another planned community in Florida. Just as DPZ's vision for the town as a whole entails a varied alternation of streets, blocks, and open spaces, the individual houses offer bright, open rooms and cozier, receded spaces, all efficiently arranged to flow seamlessly into one another.

OPPOSITE

A wall in the study of a Hugh Newell Jacobsen home is lined with the architect's trademark cubic shelving, corralling the extensive library of its art-collecting residents.

133

Even in Windsor's most modern homes, those intimate areas provide an opportunity to balance minimal, streamlined forms with the organic warmth of wood, as in a Brad Lynch–designed study where a library is concealed behind a partial wall of African acacia. "We didn't want to enclose the rooms, but we wanted to privatize that space," says the architect. The result is a functional, modern office that, when viewed from anywhere else in the house, appears as nothing more than a wall of rich wood at one end of the wide-open living room.

It's a balancing act that no one employs more deftly than Hugh Newell Jacobsen. In his Windsor projects, walls of wooden shelves in his trademark cubic pattern provide an appealing foil to the clear, expansive sight lines throughout the rest of the house. These rooms are where you'll find some of the most clever space-saving techniques too: besides the obvious storage provided by the shelves, Jacobsen's studies offer up thoughtful details like a television discreetly tucked behind millwork and pocket doors that slide open and shut depending on the level of seclusion one wants. "Everything is pushed back behind almost invisible doors and the rest is just art and color and fabrics—the stuff that really defines the palette," explains Simon Jacobsen of his father's strategic expressions of minimalism.

Look closely at many of these spaces, too, and you just might find a hidden bar awaiting a cocktail party or a quiet nightcap. Some are incorporated within built-in shelves, some stashed behind doors that open to reveal an exuberant burst of blue lacquer or mirrored shelves housing highball glasses and shakers.

The town's most showstopping study may be (perhaps unsurprisingly) in the Weston's own home, where a corner room that less enterprising designer-client teams night well have overlooked has been transformed into a beguiling hideaway with bamboo-clad walls, sexy, low-slung furniture, and Chinese parasols hung like art. It's the ultimate expression of Stefanidis's wish for the Weston residence to avoid easy design categorization. Here, he's produced a delightful surprise in a home full of unique pairings—all tucked into the most unexpected place in the house. The most interesting homes, after all, are always the ones that offer up a sense of discovery at every turn.

OPPOSITE
Jacobsen used deadhead cypress harvested from the floor of the Apalachicola River for the study's paneling.

OVERLEAF
Tucked into a corner of the Jacobsen house, the study is a pocket of warmth on the otherwise clean-lined, white-walled ground floor.

OPPOSITE

In this study, interior designer Liz Eubank swathed the walls, ceiling, and cabinetry in a deep blue lacquer, which she balanced with rattan furniture and blinds.

ABOVE

A Kartell Louis Ghost chair by Philippe Starck is a modern contrast to an antique desk and a dark wood artwork in an Olivia O'Bryan–designed office.

OVERLEAF

Designer Kim Zimmerman brightened up a dark, small-windowed corner room with a coating of salmon-hued lacquer paint. A reflective high gloss on the ceiling and trim adds dimension.

PRECEDING PAGES
Alessandra Branca opted for a tried-and-true palette of blue and white with woven wicker for this family room in an oceanfront house.

OPPOSITE
In a guest suite designed by Branca, French doors open to a shared outdoor space, giving visitors a taste of the courtyard experience.

ABOVE
Bamboo shelves house books and beach treasures in an oceanfront house decorated by Branca.

OVERLEAF
For a study off of the primary bedroom in the Westons' house, John Stefanidis channeled a tiki lounge, swathing the walls in bamboo and using parasols as décor.

PRECEDING PAGES
In a family room with furniture covered in Alessandra Branca's Casa Branca textiles, doors open to a boardwalk leading down to the beach.

ABOVE
In the family room of designer Britt Taner's home, Colefax and Fowler's iconic Bowood chintz gets a contemporary update paired with abstract modern art, a Lucite table, and Edward Wormley chairs reissued by Baker.

OPPOSITE
Taner covered the sofa and walls in the same pattern for an enveloping effect; the wicker table and stools were found at a vintage store.

Bars

Of course, no good party—or, some might say, no good family gathering, both commonplace at Windsor—is complete without a well-stocked bar. Unsurprisingly, the liquor cabinets here, it seems, are always full, with bar tables, carts, and caddies standing at the ready for a predinner spritz or end-of-the-evening nightcap. After all, who knows when someone might drop by?

ABOVE
Naoto Fukasawa's Grande Papilio armchair and ottoman in mustard yellow add a pop of color to the modern living area in a Brad Lynch–designed home.

OPPOSITE
Two partial walls of African acacia divide the Lynch home's ground floor; tucked behind one is a study with a modular shelving system.

RIGHT

In the study of a Hugh Newell Jacobsen home, a Barcelona daybed by Le Corbusier stands in front of built-in cubic shelves.

OVERLEAF

In a more traditional take on built-in bookshelves, an antique oil painting is surrounded by leather-bound volumes and collectible porcelain in the family room of a Merrill, Pastor & Colgan house.

156

Bedrooms and Bathrooms

Windsor was born as a place for its founding family to host—and by all accounts, Hilary Weston is the consummate hostess, attuned to every guest's needs right down to the bedsheets, which, an admiring John Stefanidis once proclaimed to *AD*, are "the best linens I've ever seen." Even after the inhabitants of Windsor began to branch out beyond the Westons' own family and friends, that attitude prevailed (as reflected in the Alessandra Branca–designed guest suites, conceptualized to give even short-term visitors a taste of the full Windsor experience). In keeping with this spirit of hospitality, bedrooms in the community are not only oases where their owners can retire after a full day of golf, polo, or a long walk on the beach, but opportunities to extend that same sense of divine comfort to overnight visitors. Master suites are sumptuously inviting, yes, but so, too, are the secondary—and, in many cases, tertiary, and more—bedrooms. At Windsor, guest rooms are no afterthought—they, too, are part of the master plan.

"When we built the house, we went through the process with a kind of 'extreme future' mentality," says Britt Taner, who had envisioned, when her daughters were mere preteens, spaces they might one day return to with spouses, children, and any other loved ones in tow. With Wheeler Kearns Architects, Taner devised a suite of guest rooms above her home's garage to serve this purpose.

Taner's longsighted view is not unusual at Windsor, where expanding families happily returning to the roost has been the impetus for many a renovation or "upgrade" of a house: "My children started visiting and then they had children," says Susan Zises Green by way of explaining her recent move to a larger home. "I would have put them up in the guest suites, but my son said, 'We're a family, we belong under one roof.'"

Or, as many Windsor residents interpret it, under a few clustered roofs or connected gables. Separate and semi-separate guesthouses are common in the community. "The owners have children and grandchildren who they wanted to come and stay, but they didn't want to be on top of each other," says Simon Jacobsen of the numerous guesthouses his firm has designed at Windsor, often set across a courtyard from the owners' houses. "So there are communal gathering places, but for the most part, relatives and friends are quartered apart from the main house. When the sun goes down, everybody goes back to a different home."

It's an idyllic iteration of gracious hosting, a deft way to enable open-door policies without risking guest fatigue. That is to say, the old expression about guests and fish (going bad after three days) doesn't apply here. "You sort of create this little village on the property," says Clemens Bruns Schaub. "That way everyone can have their own little space."

Besides making for far pleasanter relationships between host and guest, this approach creates the opportunity for a continuation of the community's architecture on a smaller scale. In many cases, breezeways and courtyards connect multiple dwellings on a single property, providing the same sense of spontaneous discovery even within one lot—and allowing for multiple bedrooms to open up to courtyards, gardens, or bodies of water. After all, there may be no more coveted guest amenity than an ocean view.

And yes, Windsor's detail-oriented ethos applies to bathrooms as well. Call it an extreme extension of the DPZ model, but if part of New Urbanism's theory is a pleasing, human-centric scale, it stands to reason that it would apply to personal comfort—even in a space as private as the bath. And, as no square inch of these homes is overlooked, good design continues there too. Freestanding tubs abound, often enticingly set against a window with a view or underneath a showstopping artwork (or both, if you're lucky). There are the expected lovely swaths of Carrara marble and subway tile, but also more unusual materials, like Thomas Hamel's pairing of limestone walls and granite floor topped with an antique carpet, or Patricia Davis Brown's brass riff on industrial piping, designed in collaboration with the owner. "We wanted a bit of Old World feel," says Brown. "I think it just draws you in."

Draw you in these spaces do, an impressive feat for a water closet. More often than not, there's an ocean vista, a verdant courtyard, or an artful seating area mere footsteps away—and yet there's a certain allure to a freestanding tub or waterfall shower. Within the context of their high-design homes, the bathrooms at Windsor are often a reminder that, for a sense of relaxing escape, sometimes simplicity is best.

OPPOSITE

Hugh Newell Jacobsen designed cubic takes on canopy beds (and coordinating nightstand and shelves) to frame two Ellsworth Kelly drawings hung on the terra-cotta-colored walls of a guest bedroom.

ABOVE

A sculpture by Deborah Butterfield stands in dramatic profile before Jacobsen's trademark windows.

OVERLEAF

In a bedroom designed by Kevin Dumais, a palette of soft, soothing hues keeps the focus on the view of palm trees out the window, balanced by a trio of works from Betty Merken's Illumination *series above the bed.*

PRECEDING PAGES

In the master bedroom of the Westons' own oceanside home, John Stefanidis deftly created a balance between decorative formality and beachfront ease; a breezy muslin bed canopy and lace-painted walls soften an assortment of fine antiques under an airy vaulted ceiling.

ABOVE

Gauzy hangings on the canopy bed in a second-floor bedroom impart a dreamy, ethereal feel.

OPPOSITE

The bedroom's floor-to-ceiling windows afford generous views of the courtyard below.

OVERLEAF

This bedroom in an Olivia O'Bryan and Merrill, Pastor & Colgan house has easy access to the pool and outdoor dining area—and curtains to draw when privacy is desired.

RIGHT

John Stefanidis carried through the bamboo wall treatment from the adjacent study into a guest room at the Westons' home but covered the remaining walls in a stenciled motif of his own design. A cherry grosgrain trim on the canopy hangings and chair pillows adds a crisp, buoyant note.

OVERLEAF

Curtains in a large-scale indigo print frame the ocean view out the French doors of this bedroom in a house by Clemens Bruns Schaub. The Antonio Citterio armchair for B&B Italia provides a perfect perch.

ABOVE
A desk in the guest room of an Olivia O'Bryan–designed house does double duty as a nightstand.

OPPOSITE
Grouped together and hung on textural grass cloth, small wicker-framed mirrors make a whimsical statement in a bedroom in one of the Windsor guest suites by Alessandra Branca.

OVERLEAF
For the Roman shades in the guest bedroom of Britt Taner's current Windsor house, she repurposed the Brunschwig & Fils Palm House fabric that she had used for drapes in a former home.

PAGES 182–83
Combining an electric-yellow fabric with glossy white walls, floor, ceiling, and four-poster beds, Kim Zimmerman created an exceptionally light and bright guest bedroom.

ABOVE

Cole & Son's Acquario wallpaper creates the effect of a chic underwater world in this guest bedroom designed by Leah Muller.

OPPOSITE

A popular tropical motif—the pineapple—gets a toned-down treatment in an elegant, neutral guest bedroom designed by Kim Zimmerman.

OVERLEAF

Cole & Sons' Woods wallpaper transforms a guest bedroom with bunk beds in this Hugh Newell Jacobsen home into a fantastical treehouse.

PAGES 188–89

A bedroom designed by Susan Smith at one of the smaller-scale Windsor Park Residences opens onto a shaded porch clad in warm teak.

Powder Rooms

If the bathrooms in bedroom suites are designated as soothing, spa-like escapes, powder rooms are places where designers can have a little more fun, enveloping walls in bright colors and playful patterns so that even a trip to powder one's nose at a party is sure to be a memorable experience.

OPPOSITE

With its limestone walls, granite floor, and marble tub, this Thomas Hamel–designed bathroom evokes the feel of a Roman bath; a vintage rug adds warmth.

ABOVE

Mirrored cabinet doors framing the window open up the space and reflect abstract works by Tony Tuckson.

OVERLEAF

Designer Patricia Davis Brown worked with the owner to conceive this brass-and-marble bathroom, a lavish reimagining of an industrial style.

OPPOSITE

*Designer Kevin Dumais created
an extra-long vanity to fit the
proportions of this long, narrow
bathroom; a bright David Dreben
photograph on the far wall serves
as a focal point.*

ABOVE

*The unconventional placement of
a bright painting above the exterior
door draws the eye up toward
the high ceiling in a bathroom
designed by Rod Mickley.*

OPPOSITE

A strategically placed painting in an Olivia O'Bryan–designed bathroom creates a dramatic "view" from the tub.

ABOVE

Leah Muller adds a dash of texture to an all-white bathroom with a woven-seagrass stool. The tub is positioned for sweeping views.

OVERLEAF

Freestanding soaking tubs are popular at Windsor; they exude a sense of relaxing calm.

Pools, Terraces, Verandas, and Courtyards

If anything should have become clear throughout these pages, it's that it is virtually impossible to talk about any *interior* rooms in the houses at Windsor without making constant reference to the outdoors. "DPZ believes—as do I—that the design of your home should encompass architecture, landscaping, and interiors," says Alessandra Branca. "This is especially important where your public and private lives intersect."

The outdoor spaces play the most significant role in unifying these two worlds. It's a testament to Windsor's planning that public and private space can be so deftly interwoven—with nary a towering security gate or menacing wall separating them. Instead, it's the architecture that creates the boundaries.

"Windsor gives you the opposite of the typical suburban model where you find a lot, you put an X in the lot, and you put the house in the middle," says Peter Moor. "Windsor is sort of like a centrifuge—you get the lot and you spin it and you let all the buildings go to the edges." It's a strategy that effectively maximizes space within the footprint of the lots, providing a satisfying balance of open spaces and more tucked-away rooms (like the dens and studies at the homes' corners), with the center courtyard as both a visual connector and a naturally secluded private garden.

"Most people want a garden all the way around, but if you push the buildings to the outer edge, then you can create these courtyards and inner gardens that are so special," says Thomas Hamel. Those courtyards are Windsor's most defining characteristic—and to many residents and designers, the most important (and beloved) part of their homes.

So much so that it's often the first step in an architectural plan. "Usually we begin our design by deciding where on the lot the sun and the breeze create the best courtyard," says Clemens Bruns Schaub. "And then you kind of wrap the house around it. So it's really the outdoors first and the house second."

Like the rooms that surround them, these courtyards are unified in concept yet stylistically diverse. A poolside designed by Amanda Lindroth is lined with lattice and outfitted with rattan chairs and a retro umbrella in tropical blue fabric—a setting that suggests the backdrop of a Slim Aarons photo. A Moor, Baker home, meanwhile, exudes a vaguely Moorish style with minimal riffs on ogee arches leading into a gravel-lined piazza with minimal landscaping. A Thomas Hamel courtyard takes inspiration from Bali, with low-slung daybeds, pagoda-style rooflines, and swaying palms.

Here, too, is where the importance of landscape design comes into play. Not only do the plantings enhance the architecture but they often quite literally merge with it: shrubs make up exterior walls, fronds frame doorways, trees gracefully flank pathways, wisteria and ivy and bougainvillea encase exterior columns to soften their lines. After three decades, the gardens of Windsor's homes are in varying stages of maturity, with some of the oldest homes appearing nestled into their landscape, while plantings at the newer ones continue to grow into their surroundings.

As always, on every property, there are moments of surprise: a bubbling fountain at the end of a long, narrow stretch of grass, a table clustered with topiaries under a roof overhang, a fireplace tucked at the end of a breezeway or under a stone-paved arcade.

And while these courtyards are visually intoxicating—and perfectly, painstakingly concocted—they are never ostentatious. Windsor code, ever thoughtful, steers architects toward quieter displays of leisure, a refreshing alternative to the oversized pools at many vacation villages. Even grandly sized courtyards, bordered by complementary-scaled buildings, retain a proportion that keeps them from feeling grandiose. Often, the outdoor space is divided into a variety of connecting plazas, cloisters, and arcades, with designated arrangements—seats around a fire pit, a long dining table, a water feature—for each.

That's not to say, of course, that there aren't showstoppers. The minimal, covered patios of one Schaub-designed house appear to hover atop a crescent-shaped pool, a chain of concrete blocks providing a path across the water to the grass. The far side of a patio on another appears as an islet between pool and inlet, a dramatic setting for a sculptural fire pit with chairs facing the water beyond—or the house.

Indeed, the best part of being outside at Windsor may well be the views of the homes themselves. "We always try to have our homes look at water or over water," says Simon Jacobsen—and not only for the view it affords from the inside. "That's an important visual element because having those reflections in the pool at night is so wonderful."

After all, the houses here, ultimately, are art—to the extent that, as Scott Merrill says, "it's probably one of the only places where people actually want to see the empty lot next to them developed—because it makes the place better."

That may well be the best endorsement of the joint vision of the Westons and DPZ: Windsor as an ever-evolving work of art, a community where visitors can at once feel right at home and intoxicatingly transported.

"The minute I passed through those gates, I felt like I was in another world," reflects the design editor and stylist Robert Rufino, who visited for a shoot a decade ago and was instantly transfixed. "I didn't know where I felt like I was, but I just wanted to wear white linen pants and play tennis and then sit on the porch and sip iced tea." And why wouldn't you, in such a setting?

OPPOSITE

A pergola extending from the eaves of this house creates a sheltered alcove for a table and chairs.

OVERLEAF

This spacious courtyard has room for multiple seating areas around a long, blue-tiled pool.

ABOVE
Weathered wood furniture, antique vases, and a plaster wall lend texture to a corner of a courtyard designed by Olivia O'Bryan.

OPPOSITE
Floor pillows and daybeds are arrayed around an antique carved-wood fireplace surround in this Olivia O'Bryan–designed pool pavilion.

OPPOSITE

Grass-lined pavers in a checkerboard pattern break up the brick patio in the courtyard of this home.

ABOVE

Faux-bois demilune tables hold an array of potted plants at the entrance to the house.

OVERLEAF

Aubergine doors and trim at a house by Scott Merrill of Merrill, Pastor & Colgan are a departure from the more customary pale pastels.

PRECEDING PAGES
*Vines climb an elongated pergola
in the courtyard of a home by
Merrill, Pastor & Colgan. The far
arcade houses an outdoor fireplace.*

OPPOSITE
*Thomas Hamel drew inspiration
from Indonesia for the courtyard
and interior façade at this house
designed by Clemens Bruns Schaub.*

ABOVE
*Hamel designed the roof over
the poolside daybed to mimic a
pagoda, just one of many Asian
influences throughout.*

POOLS, TERRACES, VERANDAS, AND COURTYARDS   217

ABOVE

The stainless-steel furniture in the courtyard of a Hugh Newell Jacobsen house was designed by the architect; climbing bougainvillea adds softness.

OPPOSITE

A pavilion furnished with daybeds appears to float above the swimming pool in the courtyard of a home by Clemens Bruns Schaub.

ABOVE
The pool pavilion at Britt Taner's family home reflects the barn style of the main house on a smaller scale.

OPPOSITE
In the courtyard of a home that Brad Lynch designed for a South American family, the towering outdoor fireplace hides a traditional Argentine grill behind it.

OVERLEAF
Though Windsor's code prohibits long bands of windows on its exterior façades, Brad Lynch had no such restriction for the courtyard-facing walls.

ABOVE
A pared-back take on a pool pavilion at a Hugh Newell Jacobsen–designed house shades an assortment of furniture designed by the architect.

OPPOSITE
Jacobsen's graceful spiral staircase is visible across the courtyard, beneath the architect's modern spin on Bermuda shutters.

OVERLEAF
At another Jacobsen-designed home, the courtyard—with a sculpture by Lady Pixie Shaw—acts as a central gathering place for family members staying in the guesthouses rimming the property.

OPPOSITE

At a home designed by Vigneault & Hoos, the courtyard is lush with mature planting, which ensconces an outdoor dining area.

ABOVE

The pool pavilion at the same home appears nestled among its surrounding palm trees.

OVERLEAF

When lit up at dusk, a pool pavilion by Clemens Bruns Schaub casts its reflection in the aquamarine pool beside it.

OPPOSITE
In the daytime, slatted shutters let breezes pass through the pavilion while keeping it shaded from sun.

ABOVE
A second pavilion at the other end of the pool mirrors the one attached to the home and provides a visual anchor at the end of the property.

OVERLEAF
The far pool pavilion affords a sweeping view of the golf course's undulating hills.

ABOVE

Sculptural brackets support a cantilevered balcony on a home by Moor, Baker & Associates, where bougainvillea adorns the walls.

OPPOSITE

Ivy climbs the columns outside a Rob Southern–decorated home. The minimal patio furniture is by Janus et Cie.

OVERLEAF

In the courtyard at a Clemens Bruns Schaub home, outdoor seating surrounds a central fire pit and a pair of mature palms provide shade.

PRECEDING PAGES

On the opposite side of the Schaub courtyard, an extended eave shades an orchid-topped antique wood table.

OPPOSITE

At another Schaub home, ivy in a lattice pattern decorates a dividing wall; pale blue shutters reflect the hue of the pool.

ABOVE

An antique fountain framed in greenery is the focal point at the far end of a narrow courtyard lawn.

ABOVE
The unconventional outdoor furnishings at a home designed by Amanda Lindroth, who says, "I don't believe in outdoor furniture," include two peacock chairs and a seashell-motif table.

OPPOSITE
Wicker lounge chairs and a scalloped umbrella poolside at the Lindroth-designed home have a retro resort look.

OVERLEAF
Classical columns and a symmetrical layout give the central courtyard of this home by Merrill, Pastor & Colgan—with drought-resistant landscape design by Dan Ford—the feel of an ancient Roman atrium.

PAGES 250–51
In another Merrill, Pastor & Colgan–designed home, blue beams in the passageway to the pool echo the color of the pool and the sky.

ABOVE
Kevin Dumais proves that a sliver of outdoor space can become an inviting oasis with the addition of a pergola and climbing vines.

OPPOSITE
At an early Windsor home designed by Scott Merrill in the Charleston single-house style, the side yard's long loggia is broken up with planters in assorted sizes and softened by climbing morning glory.

OVERLEAF
A riff on an ogee arch frames the quiet courtyard of a Moor, Baker house.

PAGES 256–57
At the same Moor, Baker house, Olivia O'Bryan grouped casual rattan furniture in front of a covered outdoor fireplace.

OPPOSITE

Clemens Bruns Schaub designed this striking modern home—a veritable sculpture itself—to house an extensive art collection.

ABOVE

The home's pool house, accessible across a series of concrete stepping-stones, appears to float on the reflecting pool.

OVERLEAF

Outside a home by John Brenner, chairs encircle a fire pit set between the home's pool and a lake, affording sweeping views of the golf course beyond.

PRECEDING PAGES
On a waterside covered porch designed by Olivia O'Bryan, a swing invites breezy relaxation.

ABOVE
The beach beckons from beyond a boardwalk outside an oceanfront house decorated by Alessandra Branca.

OPPOSITE
The view of palms, dunes, and sea from the second floor of an oceanfront house.

OPPOSITE

An aqua ceiling and white-painted wicker furniture upholstered in a pretty floral print give the porch at the Westons' Stefanidis-designed home the feel of eternal summer.

ABOVE

The Westons' porch makes an ideal spot for afternoon tea overlooking the ocean.

OVERLEAF

Outside an early Windsor house by Clemens Bruns Schaub, a cerulean pool appears to extend to the ocean beyond; seafoam railings and trim reflect the sea's lighter hues.

IN MEMORY OF W. GALEN WESTON

Acknowledgments

First, thank you to the many talented architects and designers who were so generous in sharing their incredible work and recounting the stories behind these beautiful homes. Thank you to the immensely stylish residents of Windsor for allowing us a peek into your most personal spaces, to the team there (Jane, Erin, Laurin) for your help on questions big and small, and of course, to the Westons for conceiving such a gem and bringing it to life. Thank you to the Vendome team for entrusting me with this delightful project and guiding me so deftly along the way: to Mark for your vision, Jessica for capturing Windsor's essence in photographs, Jackie for making sure I sounded good, and Celia for bringing it all together so beautifully on the page. It was a joy to work with each of you. Thank you to my team at *House Beautiful* for indulging this endeavor and always championing me. Finally, thank you to the people who support me the most: my parents, who I know will truly read every word, my siblings, and the most wonderful friends, each of whom inspire me daily, and Thomas for constant counsel and encouragement.

HADLEY KELLER

This book would not have been possible without the expert vision of Mark Magowan and his amazing team at Vendome Press. Thank you to editor Jackie Decter and designer Celia Fuller for making the book flawless and artistically captivating, and to authors Hadley Keller and James Reginato, whose words bring Windsor to life.

Thank you to my husband, Gerard Glynn, for the endless support and sound advice; to my daughter, Keira Glynn, for inspiring me to be the best person I can; to my mother, Gail Klewicki, my first and best photo assistant, who has helped me on over 120 shoots at Windsor; and to my father, Raymond Klewicki, for picking up Keira from school every day.

I am deeply grateful to the people who help make my photography look good and support me, including Mary Juckiewicz, Krissy Costea, Mike Warnock, Frank Martucci, and Kerry Doyle-Waite.

Thank you to the founders of Windsor, Hilary and W. Galen Weston, for envisioning and establishing this community, which is an architectural photographer's dream. I'd also like to thank the wonderful team at Windsor: Laurin Lott Pohl, Jane Smalley, and Betsy Hanley. Thank you to all of the architects, designers, and homeowners at Windsor, and especially to my clients Ashley Waddell and Courtney Harris of Olivia O'Bryan Inc.; Clemens Bruns Schaub and Christine Pokorney; Peter Moor and Chris Baker; Scott Merrill; Leah Muller; and Liz Eubank.

JESSICA KLEWICKI GLYNN

OPPOSITE
Visitors' first sight of Windsor is the stately allée of live oaks that lines the approach to the community.

Beachside: Windsor Architecture and Design
First published in 2021 by The Vendome Press
Vendome is a registered trademark of The Vendome Press, LLC

NEW YORK
Suite 2043
244 Fifth Avenue
New York, NY 10001

LONDON
63 Edith Grove
London,
SW10 0LB, UK

www.vendomepress.com

Distributed in North America by Abrams Books
Distributed in the United Kingdom, and the rest of the world, by Thames & Hudson

ISBN 978-0-86565-403-7

PUBLISHERS: Beatrice Vincenzini, Mark Magowan, and Francesco Venturi
EDITOR: Jacqueline Decter
PRODUCTION DIRECTOR: Jim Spivey
DESIGNER: Celia Fuller

Library of Congress Cataloging-in-Publication Data
available upon request

Printed and bound in China by 1010 Printing International Ltd.

FIRST PRINTING

PHOTO CREDITS

All photographs by Jessica Klewicki Glynn, with the exception of the following:

Carmel Brantley: pp. 14–15, 17, 18–19, 20, 34, 35, 59, 63, 88, 89, 90–91, 98, 99,
152 top left, 160, 163, 168–69, 190 bottom right, 191 top left, 197, 246, 247, 266, 267
Paul Costello / OTTO: pp. 64, 65, 146–47, 174–75
Nick Johnson: pp. 108, 109, 176–77
Joshua McHugh: pp. 166–67, 196
William Abranowicz / Art + Commerce: pp. 114, 115, 216, 217, 192

PAGE 1
*The inviting entryway of a
home decorated by Olivia
O'Bryan offers a glimpse of
the bougainvillea outside.*

PAGES 2–3
*An eclectic array of artworks
in an Olivia O'Bryan–designed
home adds warmth to minimal
architecture by Moor, Baker
& Associates.*

PAGES 4–5
*With its soaring ceiling, this living
room in a house designed by
architect Hugh Newell Jacobsen
makes a unique backdrop for Rob
Pruitt's Autograph Collection.*

PAGES 6–7
*The ocean-facing veranda of
a home decorated by Steven
Gambrel offers up plenty of
seating for guests on Kingsley Bate
furniture with a nautical palette.*

PAGE 8
*The airy entryway of a Merrill,
Pastor & Colganand Olivia
O'Bryan–designed home opens
onto an extensive vista of the golf
course beyond.*

PAGE 10
*Covered in mosaic tile, this
corner of a courtyard is
an inviting setting for an
alfresco meal.*